❈ SISTER ❈

ARIEL BOOKS

**Andrews McMeel
Publishing**
Kansas City

Design by BTDnyc
Illustrations © 2002 Stephanie Dalton Cowan
Edited by Mary Rodarte

ISBN: 0-7407-1492-9
Library of Congress Catalog Card Number:
2001096656

SISTER

SISTER

*W*e spoke in whispers as children do,

And now it was I—

and then it was you.

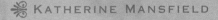 KATHERINE MANSFIELD

*O*ur sisters . . . our mirrors:
our images
of who we are and of who
we can dare to become.

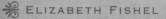 ELIZABETH FISHEL

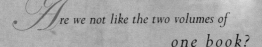

*A*re we not like the two volumes of
one book?

❀ MARCELINE
DESBORDES-VALMORE

*W*e wove a web in childhood,

A web of sunny air.

 CHARLOTTE BRONTË

The only one
I could wholly, totally confide in,
lives in the same house with me,
and not only never has,
but never will,
leave me one secret to tell her.

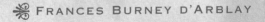 FRANCES BURNEY D'ARBLAY

The bond that joined us lay deeper
than outward things;
The rivers of our souls spring from
the same well!

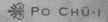 PO CHÜ-I

We talked as Girls do—
Fond, and late—
We speculated fair, on every subject . . .

 EMILY DICKINSON

*S*o closely **interwoven** have been our lives, our purposes and experiences that, separated, we have a **feeling** of incompleteness.

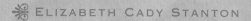 ELIZABETH CADY STANTON

Like—but oh how different!

 WILLIAM WORDSWORTH

*I*f the family were a fruit, it would be
an orange, a circle of sections, held together
but separable—each segment distinct.

✿ LETTY COTTIN POGREBIN

*T*o you alone I venture to complain;

From others hourly strive to hide my pain.

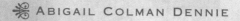 ABIGAIL COLMAN DENNIE

I my Companions see
In You, another Me.

 THOMAS TRAHERNE

Even the conjugal tie is beneath the fraternal. Children of the same family, the same blood, with the same first associations and habits, have some means of enjoyment in their power, which no subsequent connections can supply.

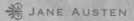 JANE AUSTEN

. . . *the* most
competitive relationship
within the family . . .

 MARGARET MEAD

They had grown up together,—
A world unto themselves.
All else was bare,—
A desert to them and an unknown sea . . .

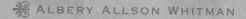 ALBERY ALLSON WHITMAN

. . . the unison of well-tuned hearts . . .

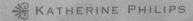

Comparison is a death knell to sibling harmony.

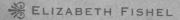 ELIZABETH FISHEL

$\mathcal{W}$ho laughed and played with me

in childhood hours

Full many a summer day and told me tales

Of fairy lore . . .

✤ GEORGE MARION
MCCLELLAN

You are like me,

But you are not I.

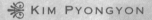KIM PYONGYON

. . . the most sublime of all affections,
because it is founded on principle, and
cemented by time.

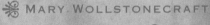 MARY WOLLSTONECRAFT
GODWIN

. . . my only sister, . . .

Do not mistakenly regard her as
of common stock;
She is the *heart-taker* among the crowds,
Radiant as a rainbow, she is
more beautiful than angels.

 SONGS OF MILAREPA

$\mathscr{E}$ven when you are old, the escapades
of our youth will revisit you!

 SAPPHO

I knew you as I know *myself.*

❧ SONG OF SOLOMON

I wish to God, *dear sister*, that you was as regular in letting me have the pleasure of knowing what passes on your side of the globe, as I am careful in endeavoring to amuse you by the account of all I see that I think you care to hear of.

❦ LADY MARY
WORTLEY MONTAGU

A shadow in the parching sun,
and a shelter
in a blustering storm . . .

 ANNE BRADSTREET

"Then I shall have a little brother!"

I exclaimed, "or else a little sister!

Oh, no, I don't want that;

I don't like little sisters!"

 SARAH BERNHARDT

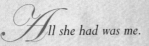

All she had was me.

All I had was her.

 BILLIE HOLIDAY

*She had come to be a friend
and companion
such as few possessed.*

 JANE AUSTEN

*O*h, the comfort, the inexpressible
comfort of feeling safe with a person;
having neither to weigh thoughts nor
to measure words but to pour them all out,
just as it is, chaff and grain together.

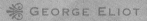 GEORGE ELIOT

$\mathcal{Y}$ou knew every quirk of my soul,

you felt even the slightest

twitch of a nerve;

with one look you could

read me right through,

as none other has ever been able . . .

❧ JOHANN WOLFGANG

VON GOETHE

For there is no friend like a sister
In calm or stormy weather.

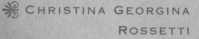 CHRISTINA GEORGINA
ROSSETTI

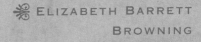

$\mathcal{W}$e are so unlike each other,

Thou and I, that none could guess

We were *children* of one mother.

❦ ELIZABETH BARRETT
BROWNING

I recognize how crucial
my relationship with my sisters
is in the definition of myself.

❧ BARBARA MATHIAS

Today is far from Childhood—
But up and down the hills
I held her hand the tighter—
Which shortened all the miles—

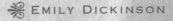 EMILY DICKINSON

$\mathcal{Y}$our life and mine are just

two threads

in this eternal canvas.

They diverge, converge, and interweave

with each other,

then diverge and converge again

until the fabric is complete.

❈ KAHLIL GIBRAN

*W*e cannot destroy kindred:
our chains stretch a little sometimes,

but they n e v e r break.

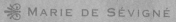 MARIE DE SÉVIGNÉ

One soul was ours, one mind,

one heart devoted.

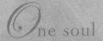 HARTLEY COLERIDGE

. . . let us enjoy each other

and be sure that no rainburst or seas or

seastorm lure us to separation

before our lives end . . .

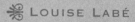 LOUISE LABÉ

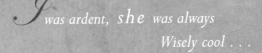

I was ardent, she was always
Wisely cool . . .

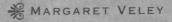

MARGARET VELEY

We twain would walk together

Through every weather . . .

✦ HENRY DAVID THOREAU

Our chang'd and mingled souls
are grown
To such acquaintance . . .

 KATHERINE PHILIPS

Shall we stick by each other

as long as we live?

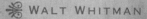 WALT WHITMAN

There are all those
early memories;
one cannot get another set; one has only those.

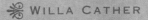 WILLA CATHER

$\mathcal{M}$y heart

has just been called back to the time

when we used to sit with our arms around

each other at the sunset hour & talk until

both our hearts felt warmer and lighter for

the pure communion of spirit.

 ANTOINETTE
LOUISA BROWN

It is the secret sympathy,
The silver link, the silken tie,
Which heart to heart and mind to mind,
In body and in soul can bind.

  SIR WALTER SCOTT

Till the last sleep,

from the blind waking at birth,

Bearing the weight of the years

between the two,

I shall find

no better thing upon the earth

Than the wilful, noble, faulty thing

which is you.

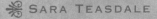 SARA TEASDALE

Our heart-strings early twined;
Some rare bond of affection . . .

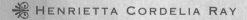 HENRIETTA CORDELIA RAY

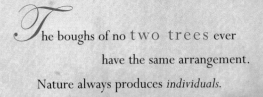

The boughs of no two trees ever
have the same arrangement.
Nature always produces *individuals*.

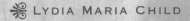

❧ LYDIA MARIA CHILD

W...

 Went about in one another's
  Clothing, bore each other's sins,
 Rose together, ere the pearly
 Tint of morn had left the heaven . . .

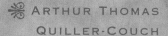

ARTHUR THOMAS
QUILLER-COUCH

We've been long together,

Through pleasant and

through cloudy weather.

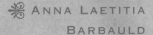 ANNA LAETITIA
BARBAULD

I cannot deny that, now I am without your company I feel not only that I am deprived of a very dear sister, but that I have lost half of myself.

 BEATRICE D'ESTE

We have been friends together
In sunshine and shade.

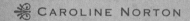 CAROLINE NORTON

*My sister! my sweet sister! if a name
Dearer and purer were, it should be
Thine.*

❊ GEORGE GORDON,
LORD BYRON

There can be no situation in life in

which the conversation of

my dear sister

will not administer some comfort to me.

❦ LADY MARY
WORTLEY MONTAGU

*W*e know one another's faults, virtues, catastrophes, mortifications, triumphs, rivalries, desires, and how long we can each hang by our hands to a bar. We have banded together under pack codes and tribal laws.

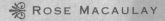 ROSE MACAULAY

You know full as well as I do the value
of sisters' **affections** to each other;
there is nothing like it in this world.

 CHARLOTTE BRONTË

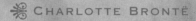

*W*e were a club, a society,
a civilization all our own.

❀ ANNETTE, CÉCILE, MARIE,
AND YVONNE DIONNE

Sticks in a bundle are

unbreakable.

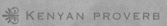 KENYAN PROVERB

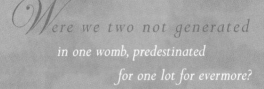

Were we two not generated

in one womb, predestinated

for one lot for evermore?

FRIEDRICH NIETZSCHE

I like a . . . *friend*
who will stand by me,
  not only when I am in the right, but when
    I am a little in the wrong.

❈ SIR WALTER SCOTT

Nobody who has not been in the interior of a family can say what the difficulties of any individual of that family may be.

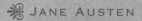

✾ JANE AUSTEN

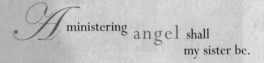
A ministering angel shall
my sister be.

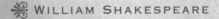
WILLIAM SHAKESPEARE

To be my best I need you

swimming beside me.

❧ MARIAH BURTON NELSON

I had a sister lovely in my sight:
Her hair was dark, her eyes were
                                    very sombre;
We sang together in the woods at night.

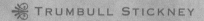 TRUMBULL STICKNEY

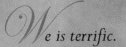 *We is terrific.*

 THE SUPREMES

*P*oliteness, that cementer of

friendship

and soother of enmities,

is nowhere so much required, and so

frequently outraged,

as in family circles.

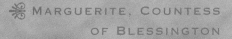 MARGUERITE, COUNTESS
OF BLESSINGTON

Heirlooms

we don't have in our family.

But stories we've got.

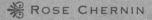 ROSE CHERNIN

I contemplate you with such

　　　　strange mixture of humility,

admiration, reverence, love, and pride.

 THEODOSIA BURR ALSTON

May the lines of love meet in your heart.

 IRISH BLESSING

My sister!

With that thrilling word

Let thoughts unnumbered wildly spring!

 MARGARET DAVIDSON

All that touches us, myself and you,

takes us together like a violin bow

that draws a single voice out of two strings.

 RAINER MARIA RILKE

We two have had such happy hours

together

That my heart melts in me to think of it.

❦ WILLIAM WORDSWORTH

Our brothers and sisters are there
with us from the dawn of our personal
stories to the inevitable dusk.

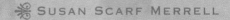 SUSAN SCARF MERRELL

If they be two*, they are* two *so*

As stiff twin compasses are two*,*

Thy soul the fixed foot, makes no show

To move, but doth, if th' other do.

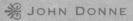 JOHN DONNE

The best and most beautiful things in the world cannot be seen or even touched. They must be felt with the heart.

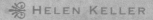

HELEN KELLER

Hard to remember our

long talks *together*;

I think of your boat pushing off in the spring.

Every three years you come for a visit;

what good is a third of a life?

 YANG WAN-LI

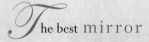 The best mirror

. . . an old friend.

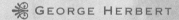 George Herbert

The human heart, at whatever age,
opens only to the heart that opens in return.

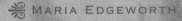 MARIA EDGEWORTH

What we remember from childhood we remember forever—permanent ghosts, stamped, imprinted, eternally seen.

※ CYNTHIA OZICK

I seek thy company
so that I may sing.

 RABINDRANATH TAGORE

Sometimes I like you,

but sometimes

I do not!

 SONGS OF MILAREPA

Come the wild weather, come sleet or come snow,
We will stand by each other, however it blow.

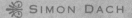 SIMON DACH

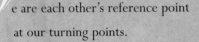

We are each other's reference point
at our turning points.

❧ ELIZABETH FISHEL

I will call my sister Nepenthe,

forgetfulness of the past,

remembrance

of childhood together . . .

 HILDA DOOLITTLE

Ye have kindred voices clear

Ye alike unfold the wing

Migrate hither, sojourn here,

Both attendant on the spring . . .

 EUENUS

Thou art the star that guides me

Along life's c h a n g i n g sea;

And whate'er fate betides me,

This heart still turns to thee.

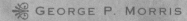 GEORGE P. MORRIS

$\mathcal{Y}$ou were born *together*,

and together

you shall be forevermore.

 KAHLIL GIBRAN

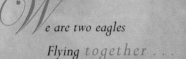

We are two eagles

Flying together . . .

 SARA TEASDALE

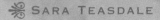

O generous-hearted sister,
In all Life's winding ways
May we have joy together!

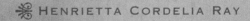 HENRIETTA CORDELIA RAY

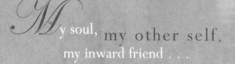

My soul, my other self,
my inward friend . . .

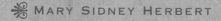

MARY SIDNEY HERBERT

NOTES

Alston, Theodosia Burr (1783–1813), "Letter," 1809

Austen, Jane (1775–1817), *Emma* (p. 36); *Mansfield Park,* 1814 (p. 20)

Barbauld, Anna Laetitia (1743–1825), "Ode to Life"

Bernhardt, Sarah (1844–1923), *Memoirs*

Blessington, Marguerite, Countess of (1789–1849), *The Repealers,* 1833

Bradstreet, Anne (1612–1672), "Meditations Divine and Mortal"

Brontë, Charlotte (1816–1855), *Retrospection* (p. 10)

Brown, Antoinette Louisa (1825–1921), "Letter to Lucy Stone"

Browning, Elizabeth Barrett (1806–1861), "Bertha in the Lane"

Cather, Willa (1873–1947)

Chernin, Rose (1903–)

Child, Lydia Maria (1802–1880)

Sévigné, Marie de (1626–1696), *Letters of Madame de Sévigné to Her Daughter and Her Friends*

Shakespeare, William (1564–1616), *Hamlet*, 1600–1601

Song of Solomon (c. 1st–2nd century)

Songs of Milarepa (11th century), "Challenge from a Wise Demoness" (p. 95); "The Meeting at Silver Spring" (p. 29)

Stanton, Elizabeth Cady (1815–1902), "Letter"

Stickney, Trumbull (1874–1904), "Mnemosyne"

The Supremes (20th century)

Tagore, Rabindranath (1861–1941), "Fireflies"

Teasdale, Sara (1884–1933), "The Flight" (p. 103); "To M" (p. 57)

Thoreau, Henry David (1817–1862), "Great Friend"

Traherne, Thomas (1637–1674), "Shadows in the Water"

Veley, Margaret (dates unknown), "A Japanese Fan"

Whitman, Albery Allson (1851–1901), "The Octoroon"

Whitman, Walt (1819–1892), "Song of the Open Road," *Leaves of Grass*, 1855–1892

Wordsworth, William (1770–1850) "Travelling" (p. 85); "Yes, It Was the Mountain Echo," 1807 (p. 16)

Yang Wan-li (c. 12th–13th century), "A Visit from Wang Hsüan-Tzu"

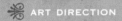 ART DIRECTION

AND DESIGN BY BTDnyc

THIS BOOK IS SET IN

PERPETUA, COPPERPLATE GOTHIC,

AND EDWARDIAN SCRIPT.